Sponges

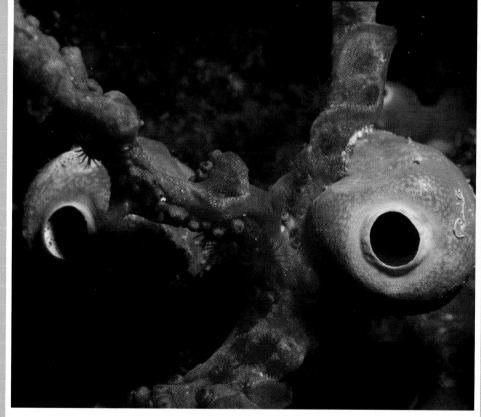

By Mary Logue

THE CHILD'S WORLD®
CHANHASSEN, MINNESOTA

Published in the United States of America by The Child's World®
PO Box 326, Chanhassen, MN 55317-0326
800-599-READ
www.childsworld.com

Content Advisers:
Jim Rising, PhD,
Professor of Zoology,
University of Toronto,
Department of Zoology,
Toronto, Ontario,
Canada, and Trudy
Rising, Educational
Consultant, Toronto,
Ontario, Canada

Photo Credits:
Cover/frontispiece: Lawson Wood/Corbis; cover corner: Corbis.
Interior: Animals Animals/Earth Scenes: 26 (Chris McLaughlin), 27 (OSF/L. Gould);
Susan Blanchet/Dembinsky Photo Associates: 7, 19, 25; Corbis: 4 (Maureen Barrymore),
16 (Pete Saloutos), 17, 18 (Kelly-Mooney Photography), 20 (Jonathan Blair);
Dembinsky Photo Associates: 8 (Jesse Cancelmo), 22 (Larry Mishkar); Stephen
Frink/Corbis: 10, 11; Marilyn Kazmers/Dembinsky Photo Associates: 6, 12, 23, 29;
Jeffrey L. Rotman/Corbis: 14, 24; Viola's Photo Visions, Inc./Animals Animals/Earth
Scenes: 9, 13, 15; Kent Wood/Photo Researchers: 5.

The Child's World®: Mary Berendes, Publishing Director

Editorial Directions, Inc.: E. Russell Primm, Editorial Director; Pam Rosenberg, Line
Editor; Katie Marsico, Assistant Editor; Matt Messbarger, Editorial Assistant; Susan
Hindman, Copy Editor; Susan Ashley, Proofreader; Peter Garnham, Terry Johnson,
Olivia Nellums, Katherine Trickle, and Stephen Carl Wender, Fact Checkers; Tim
Griffin/IndexServ, Indexer; Cian Loughlin O'Day, Photo Researcher; Linda S. Koutris,
Photo Selector

The Design Lab: Kathleen Petelinsek, Design and Page Production

Library of Congress Cataloging-in-Publication Data
Logue, Mary.
  Sponges / by Mary Logue.
    p. cm. — (Science around us)
  ISBN 1-59296-274-2 (library bound : alk. paper) 1. Sponges—Juvenile literature.
I. Title. II. Science around us (Child's World (Firm))
  QL371.6.L64 2004
  593.4—dc22   2004003669

TABLE OF CONTENTS

CHAPTER ONE

WHAT IS A SPONGE?

Sponges are all around us in our daily lives. We use them to wash our dishes, to wipe down our counters, and to clean our bodies. While most of the sponges we use today are made by humans, years ago they came only from marine animals. These animals are called sponges.

Natural sponges were once living marine animals.

Most of the sponges that people use today are synthetic sponges such as the rectangular bright pink sponge in this picture.

Natural sponges are usually oddly shaped. Synthetic sponges usually have even edges and square corners.

Scientists first thought that sponges were plants growing in the ocean. After studying them more careful-ly, they realized that these **organisms** ate food and did not have plant characteristics such as roots or leaves. Sponges were reclassified as animals. They were given the scientific name porifera.

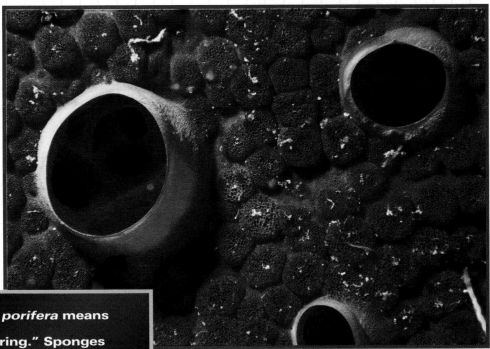

A close-up view of an orange boring
sponge shows its many pores.

The word *porifera* means
"pore-bearing." Sponges
were given this name
because they are filled with
small holes, or pores.

A sponge is a plantlike underwater

animal with pores and a tough, fibrous skeleton. To understand what

a sponge is, think of it as a big stomach. The ocean water enters a

sponge through its pores. Then the food particles in the water—

mainly bacteria—are taken in through its cells, and the filtered water

is spit out through one or more larger holes in the sponge's body.

Sponges have been around for a long time. They are the most

primitive **multicellular** animal. Porifera have lived on Earth for about 550 million to 650 million years. Sponges are found in every ocean in the world, including the cold waters of the Arctic Ocean. There are also some freshwater sponges.

Like coral, sponges help build ocean reefs. When sponges die, their skeletons add to the formation of the reef structures in the ocean. But sponges can also destroy coral when the two are fighting for space.

Coral reefs in the Caribbean Sea are home to many kinds of sponges, such as these smooth red finger sponges.

CHAPTER TWO

WHAT MAKES UP A SPONGE?

A sponge is an animal that is defined more by what it doesn't

have than by what it does have. A sponge doesn't have a head

or a mouth. It doesn't have a heart, lungs, or any internal organs.

Because a sponge is attached to the sea bottom, it has no feet. It has

no eyes, no ears, and as far as we know, no sense of smell or taste.

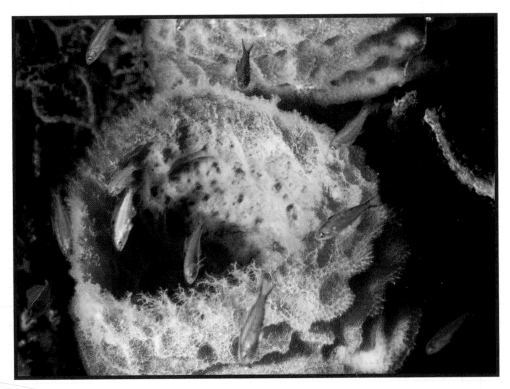

Fish swim near azure vase sponges off the coast of Belize.

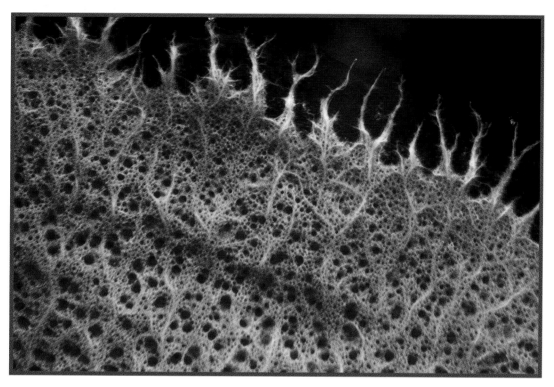

Some sponges have skeletons made of sharp, needlelike spicules.

A sponge is just one big skeleton. This skeleton can be made of soft material called spongin, or it can be as sharp and pointy as needles, which are called spicules. When the sponge is alive, the skeleton is covered with a skin that resembles leather. This skin is dotted with holes or pores. It is through these pores that the water enters the body of the sponge. The root or base of the sponge is called the holdfast.

Water enters a sponge through its pores. Then the water is pulled down canals, where nutrients and oxygen are removed. As the sponge moves water through its body, it also acts as a filter. Sponges remove about 90 percent of the bacteria from the water they filter. In doing this, sponges help keep the waters of the ocean clean.

To test whether or not sponges move water through their bodies, divers put colored dye in the bottom of a tube sponge. In just a few seconds, the colored dye came shooting out the top.

Many people enjoy scuba diving and observing sponges and other sea life.

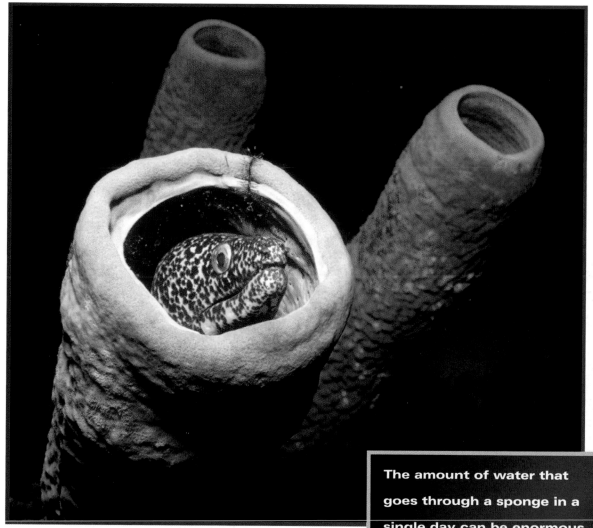

A spotted moray eel looks out of a tube sponge.

Sponges also serve as protection

and even homes for other sea creatures,

such as shrimp, crabs, and small fish.

The amount of water that goes through a sponge in a single day can be enormous. On average, a sponge pumps through its body up to 10,000 times its own volume in water. A sponge the size of a gallon of milk might pump enough water to fill a small swimming pool!

CHAPTER THREE

HOW SPONGES LIVE

Most sponges don't move around. They are permanently attached to the ocean bottom or to some object in the water. However, if they are attached to the shell of a crab, they move with the crab.

Hermit crabs sometimes use sponges for shelter and protection.

Most sponges are hermaphroditic animals. This means that they are both male and female. One sponge plays the male role and releases the sperm into the water. Another sponge acts as the female, takes in the sperm, and fertilizes its eggs. The eggs change into **larvae.** The sponge larvae are released into the ocean water. After a few days of floating in the ocean, they root and start to

A tube sponge releases its larvae into the water.

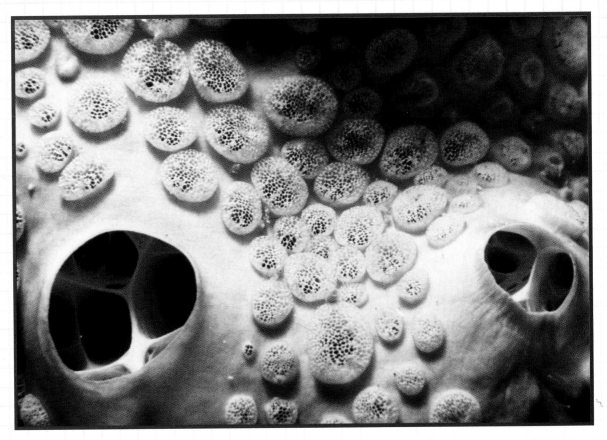

This close-up view of a sponge shows its many buds.

grow into new adult sponges. At other times of their lives, these

sponges may reverse their roles in mating.

A few sponges are **asexual.** They produce buds, which either

break off during a storm or are detached by the sponge. These buds

float around in the water until they attach themselves to the sea bot-

tom and grow into new sponges.

Sponges don't have many enemies. A few fish and sea slugs will eat them. Hawksbill turtles will also eat sponges. Many sponges contain toxic substances that keep predators away. Some marine animals take advantage of this characteristic and attach sponges to their bodies to protect themselves.

A sea slug feeds on sponges.

Scientists are studying sponges because they have been
found to contain substances that can help fight diseases.

One of the first drugs found for treating cancer—cytosine arabinoside—was found in a sponge.

Sponges have also been found to contain substances with beneficial effects. These substances might one day treat cancers or stomach problems or serve as **antibiotics.**

CHAPTER FOUR

HOW SPONGES ARE USED

Sponges have been used by people for more than 2,000 years. Until the 1800s, the Mediterranean Sea was the source for most of the sponges harvested for cleaning and other household purposes. Then suitable sponges were found in the waters off the coast of Florida and in the Caribbean Sea.

Greek sponge divers came to Florida in the early 1900s to work. At this time, sponge fishing was an important industry. The divers started to harvest sponges near the town of Tarpon Springs. However, in the 1950s,

A fleet of sponge fishing boats at harbor in Tarpon Springs, Florida, in the 1940s.

A sponge harvester strings sponges aboard a ship.

Most of the sponge fishers working in the United States today are related to those first Greek immigrant families in Tarpon Springs, Florida.

diseases and overfishing reduced the number of sponges available for harvesting. In addition, the introduction of synthetic sponges greatly reduced the demand for natural sponges.

There are probably more than 10,000 species of sponges, but only 17 are used to make household sponges. The sponges must have a skeleton made of spongin fibers. They must be **durable,** soft, and able to absorb water.

Five species of sponges are harvested in Florida. Three of these—the sheepswool sponge, the yellow sponge, and the grass sponge—make up most of the sponges sold to people.

Thousands of different kinds of sponges can be found in oceans throughout the world, but only a small number of them are suitable for use as household sponges.

A sponge diver shows off his catch.

Before World War II, (1939–1945), Florida produced about 272,000 kilograms (600,000 pounds) of sponges a year.

Recently the production has dropped to about 27,200 kilograms (60,000) pounds per year.

Sponges can be gathered from boats with hooks or by divers who cut them loose. Either way, if enough of the sponge is left, it can grow back, or regenerate. Once sponges have been gathered, they are covered and allowed to rot so that their tough skin **disintegrates.** Then they are cleaned until only the sponge skeleton remains.

Synthetic sponges have reduced the use of natural sponges for everyday household cleaning. However, marine sponges are still used for bathing, decorative painting, and cleaning windows and cars.

CHAPTER FIVE

TYPES OF SPONGES

Sponges are broken into three groups—calcareous sponges, glass sponges, and demosponges.

Calcareous sponges are the smallest group. These sponges have a skeleton made of calcium carbonate. This is the same substance that

Freshwater sponges found in the waters of Michigan.

Most calcareous sponges are dull in color but some, such as these yellow calcareous sponges, are brightly colored.

Calcareous sponges are often hard to find because they are small and sand-colored. They blend in with their environment.

clams use to make their shells. It is very

brittle and hard. These sponges tend to be smaller than 10 centime-

ters (4 inches) in diameter and are most often found in shallow

ocean waters. The classic shape for a calcareous sponge is the vase.

Glass sponges are so delicate that they often break when they are brought to the surface of the ocean.

There are about 500 species of glass sponges. They are called glass sponges because their skeletons are joined together in **intricate** patterns that resemble blown glass. Glass sponges are often very **fragile.** Some people collect them because they are so beautiful. Most of these sponges are found only in deep ocean waters.

Demosponges are the largest group of sponges, with about 9,500 species. This group includes the 150 species of freshwater sponges. Sponges that are harvested for sale are in this group. They can be found in shallow or deep water. They can be longer than

Red vase sponges can be found in the Caribbean Sea.

A tube sponge can be more than 51 centimeters (20 inches) in length. These sponges pull water in through the pores on their sides and push the filtered water out through the tops of their tubes.

1 meter (3 feet) and are often very bright in color. You can find red vase sponges in the Caribbean and blue tube sponges in the Philippines.

In 1995, carnivorous sponges no bigger than a thumbnail were discovered in caves in the Mediterranean Sea. They catch live prey on hooklike spicules at the end of long **filaments** and then eat it. It almost looks as if they are fishing.

A diver swims near large yellow tube sponges in the Cayman Islands.

Scientists who study sponges believe that there are probably some kinds of sponges that have not been discovered yet.

Scientists have studied and named thousands of species of sponges. There are probably more living in dark caves or deep crevices that have yet to be discovered. Maybe you or one of your friends will grow up to be a marine biologist. Wouldn't it be exciting to discover a new kind of sponge or other sea creature?

GLOSSARY

antibiotics (an-ti-bye-OT-iks) Antibiotics are drugs which fight infection and disease.

asexual (a-SEK-shu-uhl) Reproduction that takes place without the union of male and female cells is called asexual reproduction.

disintegrates (dis-IN-tuh-grayts) If something disintegrates, it breaks apart into small pieces.

durable (DUR-uh-buhl) Something that is durable is strong and will last for a long time.

filaments (FIL-uh-ments) Filaments are objects that are very thin and threadlike.

fragile (FRAJ-uhl) Something that is fragile can be broken easily.

intricate (IN-truh-kit) Something that is intricate is very detailed.

larvae (LAR-vee) Larvae are the immature, free-living forms of animals that will change into different, mature forms.

multicellular (muhl-tee-SEL-you-luhr) Something that is multicellular is made up of more than one cell.

organisms (OR-gan-iz-uhmz) Organisms are living things, such as plants and animals.

synthetic (sin-THET-ik) If something is synthetic, it is made by humans and isn't found in nature.

▶ When a sponge releases sperm into the water, the surrounding water will turn cloudy. It can look as if the sponge is smoking.

▶ A sponge may be as small as a grain of rice or as large as 2 meters (6 feet) across.

▶ In Florida, it is against the law to harvest sponges that are less than 13 centimeters (5 inches) in diameter. Sponge fishers there use hooks that measure 13 centimeters (5 inches) in diameter. These hooks help them make sure that they do not break the law by harvesting sponges that are too small.

▶ Sanctuaries for sponges have been established in the waters off of Everglades and Biscayne national parks in Florida.

▶ As many as 16,000 different sea creatures have been found in one loggerhead sponge. Loggerhead sponges have been known to grow to be nearly 2 meters (6 feet) in diameter.

▶ Barrel sponges can grow so large that a diver can climb into one of them.

Giant barrel sponges grow only about 1 cm (1/2 inch) per year. It is believed that some of the largest barrel sponges may be more than 100 years old.

THE ANIMAL KINGDOM

VERTEBRATES

fish

amphibians

reptiles

birds

mammals

INVERTEBRATES

sponges

worms

insects

spiders & scorpions

mollusks & crustaceans

sea stars

sea jellies

HOW TO LEARN MORE ABOUT SPONGES

At the Library

Cole, Melissa. *Coral Reefs.*
San Diego, Calif.: Blackbirch Press, 2004.

Llamas, Andreu. *Sponges: Filters of the Sea.*
Milwaukee: Gareth Stevens, 1997.

Stone, Lynn M. *Sponges: Science under the Sea.*
Vero Beach, Fla.: Rourke Publishing, 2003.

On the Web

VISIT OUR HOME PAGE FOR LOTS OF LINKS ABOUT SPONGES:
http://www.childsworld.com/links.html
Note to Parents, Teachers, and Librarians: We routinely check our Web links to make sure they're safe, active sites—so encourage your readers to check them out!

Places to Visit or Contact

CORAL SEA AQUARIUM
To see live sponges and other reef animals
850 Dodecanese Boulevard
Tarpon Springs, FL 34689
813/938-5378

THE NEW ENGLAND AQUARIUM
To see the four-story giant ocean tank that contains a model of a Caribbean reef with more than 3,000 individual corals and sponges
Central Wharf
Boston, MA 02110
617/973-5200

INDEX

About the Author

Award-winning poet and mystery writer **Mary Logue** was born and raised in Minnesota. She has written and translated many books for children, including *Dancing with an Alien*.